READY, Set, LEAD!

Harriet Hodgson and Kathy Kasten

illustrated by Penny Weber

Published in the United States by BQB Publishing
(an imprint of Boutique of Quality Books Publishing Company)
www.bqbpublishing.com

Printed in the United States of America

978-1-945448-97-3 (h)
978-1-945448-98-0 (e)
978-1-945448-99-7 (audio)

Library of Congress Control Number: 2020946442

Cover and interior illustrations: Penny Weber
Interior Design Setup: Robin Krauss, www.bookformatters.com
Editor: Andrea Bern

Dedicated to child Leaders

About the Book

Authors Harriet Hodgson and Kathy Kasten believe there is a leader inside every girl and boy. The purpose for this book is to define leadership and share stepping-stones to leadership in words kids can understand.

The authors think strong leadership begins in early childhood and that parents are a child's first leaders. According to Hodgson, "A child can be a family leader, a school leader, or a neighborhood leader. And developing leadership skills helps build self-confidence."

Kasten states, "Even from a young age, strong leadership skills can be learned through intentional, step-by-step growth and application. These skills help children use their talents and connect with others more effectively."

Although this book is aimed at young children, parents and other adults will relate to it and understand its message. Ready, Set, Lead! is a beginning—a path to leadership and life.

"What do leaders do?
And why do they do it?" you ask,
as you wonder about their daily tasks.

Leaders come in all sizes and colors.
Some are young and some are old.
They can be different-either quiet or **bold**.

Helping others is their goal,
at home and far away.
Leaders try to brighten someone else's day.

Leaders are curious folks.
They like learning new things:
How butterfiles flutter and why birds sing.

Since *patience* is needed,
leaders listen with care.
They ask for help and are willing to share.

Being **careful**
with money
is always a must,
because leaders
are people
who others trust.

8

Good leaders are **detectives**.
They keep searching for facts
that add up to kind and helpful acts.

Leaders have manners.
They say "thank you" and "please:"
three words that put others at ease.

Getting people to follow
Is an ongoing task;
Leaders persuade them or simply ask.

Leaders need teammates
to get everything done.
They make things easier and more fun.

If things aren't working,
leaders make a new plan.
They keep on saying, "I can, I can."

Checking results is part of the job,
and making hard choices is, too.
The more leaders practice,
the better they do.

Though some leaders work alone,
Most have special teams;
People who make reality from dreams.

When things don't work out,
the leaders who are strong
admit errors and say, "Oops, I was wrong."

Leaders make time
for the people they know,
to help family, faith, and friendships grow.

Kids can become leaders.
Have you thought of that?
So, it's time to put on your leadership hat.

Start learning from leaders
and why they did well.
Successful leaders have stories to tell.

Just like learning to ride a bike,
Leadership starts wobbly and s l o w.
Then you gain speed, and off you go!

Leadership happens one step at a time.
Each step moves you further ahead
and gives you reasons to jump out of bed.

Don't be afraid to ask questions.
Choose the **best** answer and then . . .
take action and try again!

Share ideas with friends and groups,
and always be yourself when you do.
Let others discover the genuine YOU.

With help from Mom or Dad,
Take a look at your neighborhood.
Pick a project, and do some good.

Offer to help in **big** ways and small.
Leave things better than before.
Make leadership fun, not a chore.

Always be honest
and do what is right.
Work on leadership with all your might.

27

Leadership is teamwork.
Instead of taking credit all the time,
credit others and let them shine.

Check the results
of your work.
Look for ways
to improve.
You will find your
leadership groove.

Good leaders get better and better,
and as they grow, they feel joy.
There's a leader inside every girl and boy.

Enjoy the leadership adventure.
Set goals and reach high-
so high you feel you can touch the sky.

Just use your special gifts.
You're good at being you.
Do your best, whatever you do.

One day you'll look in a mirror
and gasp at who you see.
"I see a leader . . . and it's me!"

About the Authors

Harriet Hodgson

Harriet Hodgson has a B.S. in Early Childhood Education from Wheelock College of Education and Human Development at Boston University, an M.A. in Art Education from the University of Minnesota, and a Certificate in Management from the American Management Association.

After 12 years in the classroom, Hodgson retired from teaching and turned to writing. A freelancer for 39 years, she is the author of thousands of print/online articles and 42 books. The award-winning author loves writing so much she writes in her sleep!

Visit www.harriethodgson.com for more information about this busy wife, mother, grandmother, great grandmother, caregiver, author, mentor, and speaker. You may also find her on Facebook and Twitter.

Kathy Kasten

Kathy Kasten is the founder and CEO of Lion Crest Leadership, LLC. She is an Accredited Advanced DISC Human Behavior Specialist with Personality Insights, Inc. and a Certified John Maxwell Team speaker, coach, and trainer.

Kasten is a contributing author for the best-selling book, *Discover Your Team's Potential.*
She has been an entrepreneur, small business owner, keynote speaker, online course creator, and worked in corporate management. She specializes in helping high achievers maximize their gifts while serving others through leadership, team building, legacy living, and effective communication. Kasten has a B.S. in Business Administration from Winona State Univerity.

She is a blessed wife, mother, and grandmother who enjoys family, cats, and music.

Visit www.lioncrestleadership.com to learn more about Kasten or find her on Facebook, LinkedIn, and Instagram.